SkillAbilities
FOR YOUTH MINISTRY

Open Doors, Open Arms

How to Reach New Youth

by Sam Halverson

ABINGDON PRESS
Nashville, Tennessee

About the Writer
Sam Halverson, an ordained elder in The United Methodist Church, has been in youth ministry for 16 years. He serves as associate minister in charge of youth ministry and young adults at Lancaster First UMC, in Lancaster, Ohio, where he lives with his wife, Kathy, and young son, Jesse. He is the author of *55 Group Building Activities for Youth* (ISBN 0-687-00528-0) as well as Sunday school curriculum and several articles.

Acknowledgments
Thanks to Mike Ratliff, Colorado; Youth Specialties, California; Sharon Meeds, Washington; Tom Hoffmann, Georgia; Rick Moser, Missouri; Howard Sublett, Arkansas; Mike Selleck, Georgia; Scott Cleaveland, Georgia; Peter Copley, Ohio; Kathy Halverson, Ohio.

SKILLABILITIES FOR YOUTH WORKERS
Open Doors, Open Arms:
How to Reach New Youth
Volume 7

ISBN 0-687-08680-9

97 98 99 00 01 02 03 04 05 06—10 9 8 7 6 5 4 3 2 1

EDITORIAL AND DESIGN TEAM
Editor: Crystal A. Zinkiewicz
Production Editor: Sheila K. Hewitt
Design Manager: Phillip D. Francis
Designer: Diana Maio
Cover Design: Diana Maio
   & Phillip D. Francis

ADMINISTRATIVE TEAM
Publisher: Neil M. Alexander
Vice President: Harriett Jane Olson
Executive Editor, Teaching and Study Resources: Duane A. Ewers
Editor of Youth Resources:
   M. Steven Games

CONTENTS

WHY DO THIS?

Why should we bother to reach new youth?

Ten reasons to bring unchurched youth into your church:

10. Bringing new youth often brings new families, adding to the growth of the church.
9. Unchurched youth are given positive peer pressure—a nice change.
8. It helps the neighborhood and community by getting kids "off the streets."
7. It promotes and provides Christian values to kids who might not otherwise have firm values.
6. It's radical—everyone else isn't doing it.
5. Evangelizing to any other youth is just moving them from one church to another.
4. It will make a real difference in the life of someone loved by God.
3. It may be the only sense of community some youth will ever get.
2. It may be the only experience of the gospel some youth will ever get.
1. Jesus told us to.

Search institute has discovered and defined 40 key assets that make it more likely for a teenager to grow up to be a physically and emotionally healthy adult. Open doors and open arms contribute to the following assets for youth who were previously unchurched:

To grow up positively and to function well in society a youth needs

A COMMUNITY THAT VALUES THE YOUTH   Asset #7
The teenager perceives that the community adults value him or her.

POSITIVE PEER INFLUENCES   Asset #15
The youth's best friends model responsible behavior.

YOUTH PROGRAMS   Asset #18
The youth is involved three hours or more per week in sports, clubs, churches, or organizations at school.

RELIGIOUS COMMUNITY   Asset #19
The teenager is involved one or more hours per week in a community of faith.

VALUES OF CARING, EQUALITY, SOCIAL JUSTICE, INTEGRITY, HONESTY, RESPONSIBILITY, AND RESTRAINT   Assets #26—31
The youth places a high value on traditional Christian values.

"The average age a person experiences religious conversion is 15.6 years. For every year older than 25 years, the odds increase exponentially against unbelievers ever becoming Christians."

(*Youthworker Update,* Volume 5, Number 2)

WHAT'S THE WORD?

In many instances the Bible illustrates the need for those outside the fellowship of believers to be welcomed and even sought after by the community of faith.

The calling of every Christian is to minister to others and to spread the good news of the gospel of Jesus Christ. That means

telling others

who don't yet know

about God's Son

and their salvation.

The following are some ways the Bible supports and promotes inclusion of the unchurched in your ministry:

God told the Israelites to

welcome the stranger

into their midst since they

too had been strangers in

the land of Egypt.

(See Exodus 22:21, 23:9 and

Leviticus 19:33-34.)

In what ways does your youth ministry program create "strangers" out of youth who are outside the church? out of newcomers?

If the stranger

is welcomed,

he or she

is no longer

a stranger.

What did the community of the Israelites do to welcome the stranger? What does your community of faith do?

"Then they also will answer, 'Lord, when was it that we saw you a . . . stranger . . . and did not take care of you?' Then he will answer them, 'Truly I tell you, just as you did not do it to one of the least of these, you did not do it to me.' And these will go away into eternal punishment, but the righteous into eternal life."

Matthew 25:44-46

Where are the youth in your community who are strangers to Christ's church? How can you take care of them? How can Jesus take care of them through you? How would you treat them if they were Christ?

"[Jesus] entered Jericho and was passing through it.
A man was there named Zacchaeus; he was a chief
tax collector and was rich. He was trying to see who
Jesus was; but on account of the crowd he could
not, because he was short in stature. So he ran ahead
and climbed a sycamore tree to see him, because he
was going to pass that way. When Jesus came to the
place, he looked up and said to him, "Zacchaeus, hurry
and come down; for I must stay at your house today."
So he hurried down and was happy to welcome him.
All who saw it began to grumble and said, "He has
gone to be the guest of one who is a sinner."
Zacchaeus stood there and said to the Lord, "Look, half
of my possessions, Lord, I will give to the poor; and if I
have defrauded anyone of anything, I will pay back
four times as much." Then Jesus said to him, "Today
salvation has come to this house, because he too is a
son of Abraham. For the Son of Man came to seek out
and to save the lost."

Luke 19:1-8

Think of Zacchaeus.

Like many youth today, he was an outsider in his community. Zacchaeus was viewed as a traitor by his own people because he collected taxes for the occupying government. He skimmed off the top of his collection for his pay. He was not trusted by his neighbors.

Jesus could have done one of three things with Zacchaeus when he met him that day.

1. He could have ignored him—in which case, Zacchaeus might never have recognized who Jesus was for him.

2. He could have ridiculed him—in which case, Zacchaeus would have recognized Jesus as the same type of person who judged him and despised him every day.

3. He could have invited him to spend time with him, allowing Zacchaeus to experience the love, forgiveness, and acceptance of the Kingdom of God.

Which do you think would make a greater impact on Zacchaeus?

Which would make a greater impact on the unchurched youth in your community?

Which is your church doing now? How?

How might people grumble as they did about Zacchaeus if unchurched youth are invited into the fellowship more intentionally?

"Go therefore and make disciples of all nations, baptizing them in the name of the Father and of the Son and of the Holy Spirit, and teaching them to obey everything that I have commanded you. And remember, I am with you always, to the end of the age."

Matthew 28:19-20

WHAT'S THE CURRENT STATUS?

Upon looking at the number of new youth who joined your church in the last year, you may (or may not) feel comfortable about how your youth ministry is evangelizing. First appearances can be deceiving though.

To determine if you are truly reaching lost and searching unchurched youth, look again at your numbers.

Count how many new youth became active who were not previously connected with another church. While ministry to all youth is important, we are doing a disservice if we are not reaching unchurched youth. If the number is low, look for more ways to reach out to the needs of the outsiders—the strangers.

Check the data

How many youth are new to your church's youth ministry program over the last year? _____

How many of those youth were not involved in a church before they came to yours? _____

How many of this year's new youth are active in your church now? _____

What brought the new youth into your youth group?

What kept the new youth coming back for more?

20 ways to let outsiders know what's happening inside your youth ministry

No matter how much you plan and how many bulletin announcements you write, it's not easy letting outsiders know what's going on inside the church. We are so used to advertising from the pulpit or through newsletters or bulletins, we forget that there are other youth who have no clue about what's happening and how they can get involved.

1 SPREAD THE NEWS BY WORD OF MOUTH FROM OTHER YOUTH

"In most of the research done on church growth, by far the largest number of people who join the church come through contacts by members with their friends and family."

(*The Inviting Church,* by Roy M. Oswald and Speed B. Leas, The Alban Institute, p. 45)

From the very first time, when Andrew ran to tell Peter, John, and James about Jesus, whom he had just met, people have been led to Christ mostly through the invitations of others. A youth is very likely to invite friends to his or her church if it is a comfortable and important place.

2 PLAN HIGH-VISIBILITY EVENTS

It's not enough that your church is known. Your youth ministry programming must be visible in the community—if those outside the church are going to see what's going on inside the church.

People need to know who you and your youth are when you are out in the community together doing service, attending concerts or movies, going to the park, enjoying a swim party, or attending a baseball game. If you have a church van, put your church name on it. A banner or flag is helpful when your group is outside somewhere. T-shirts or same-color clothing help when you are together too.

Remind your group that, especially since they are highly visible, they should be mindful that they are representatives of their church as well as of Christ.

3 ADVERTISE AT SPORTS ACTIVITIES

Football, baseball, and soccer booster clubs often print programs for which they sell advertisement space. The yearbook and school newspapers also offer advertisement for a fee. Budget some money each year to help support these programs and, at the same time, advertise your church's youth ministry. Banners made for the stadium or gym might state something like:

You're in

God's grip, Raiders!

—from First Church Youth Ministry

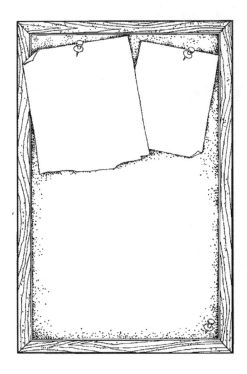

4 POST HAPPENINGS ON SCHOOL BULLETIN BOARDS

Many schools, public and private, allow community happenings to be listed on a special bulletin board. Have the youth in your youth group ask for this. Schools can grant permission when the request comes from students and not from the church.

5 OPEN THE DOORS OF THE CHURCH TO A COMMUNITY YOUTH MEETING

Often youth clubs and businesses that cater to youth in your community are looking for places to meet. Contact the scouting coordinator for your area about starting a troop. Is 4-H meeting anywhere? Is there a driver's education class looking for a large room in which to meet? Make sure that there are plenty of newsletters and informative bulletin boards on display the nights when these groups meet.

6 VISIT SCHOOL LUNCHES

Not every public school is open to this, but some schools allow adult youth leaders to visit their youth during the lunch hour. Contact the school principal, letting him or her know which youth you would like to visit. Ask your youth if they would mind your coming during their lunch (don't just show up, expecting them to welcome you to their table). While you're there, you'll meet some of their friends. And after you leave, your youth will be asked, "Who was that person who came and sat with you at lunch?"

Be careful not to do a "sales job" on the unchurched youth you may meet. You could get in trouble for this in public schools, jeopardizing future visits from you or other church leaders. Instead, let your own youth talk about their youth group and what kinds of events are coming up.

Make the Ministry Known: What's Happening?

7 START A BIBLE STUDY AT SCHOOL

Or offer to lead one that's already in place. Many schools have Christian clubs already meeting. If one is not in place at your local school, you may be able to start a Bible study after or before school. These clubs are great tools for Christian youth in introducing their unchurched friends to Christ. Adult guidance in these organizations should focus on getting these new Christians involved in a local church. You might even think about assigning a volunteer or two in your own church to one or two of these groups. Explain that they are not to recruit new youth into your church. They should let others know where they worship, though, as well as focus on getting unchurched youth into a church.

8 ATTEND SPORTS ACTIVITIES AND SIT WITH PARENTS OF YOUTH

Parents love to talk about their kids—especially when they're watching them compete on a field or in a gym. Visit the events where your own youth participate. Sit with the parents of your youth. They will, in turn, introduce you to other parents of other youth. They may even brag about what their church is doing in the youth program.

9 DO YOUTH MAILINGS

Start a monthly youth newsletter that you mail out to the youth in your church and community. This should be separate from the church newsletter or bulletin.

You can get lists of new residents in your community by contacting the Welcome Wagon or county registrar. Mail those new families your church bulletin, a youth newsletter or calendar, and a newcomer's packet with information about your church.

Once a new youth visits, make sure that he or she is put on the youth newsletter mailing list for at least six months.

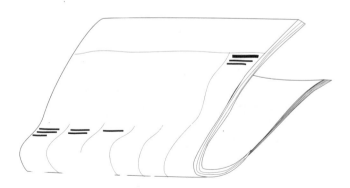

10 CREATE A WEB PAGE

There are many youth (and their parents) who spend hours cruising the world wide web. The youth ministry at your church can be made available to these people simply by keeping an updated calendar on a web page. You don't even need to have a computer at your church. Find a church member who has Internet access and can create a web page for you. Often the local Internet providers give free web space to subscribers. They might also be willing to donate a web site to the church. Some denominational offices also offer free web service to congregations.

11 CONTRIBUTE TO A CABLE COMMUNITY BULLETIN BOARD

Not many youth sit and read the community bulletin board on the cable TV screen; but many youth and their parents do surf the channels, sometimes stumbling upon an announcement that catches their eye. You can submit a free announcement through most cable companies as a public service. Make sure that the announcement is eye catching so that channel surfers will stop for a moment to read your ad.

12 INFORM THROUGH NEWSPAPERS

Does your youth group go on a summer mission trip? Do you reach out in the local community to people in need? Do you offer your community a service that is unique and important? Of course, you do! That's why your local paper might be interested in running a feature story on your youth group activities.

Contact the religion editor or feature editor at the paper on a quarterly basis and let him or her know what's coming up. An article with pictures of your youth informs the whole community about what's going on in your youth group.

13 MAKE PUBLIC SERVICE ANNOUNCEMENTS ON THE RADIO

Each radio station is required to give a certain amount of airspace for public service announcements. Contact the radio stations your youth (and even their parents) listen to and ask how you can get an announcement on the air at no charge.

14 ANNOUNCE, ANNOUNCE, ANNOUNCE

Whenever you meet with your youth, plan a few minutes to highlight the upcoming events and activities. Announce each event at least three different times before it happens. Make the announcement creative. Use drama, games, posters, and songs. Involve your youth.

15 DO SOME FUNDRAISING

When planning to do a fundraising event, choose a fundraiser that can reach people in your community who don't go to church. Door-to-door sales, car washes, races, events, and "a-thons" (bowl-a-thons, walk-a-thons, rock-a-thons) can be great fundraisers that allow your youth to be in contact with the unchurched youth of the community. These contacts inform the community of the kinds of things the group is doing—a youth mission trip, a choir tour, a local outreach, and so forth.

16 LOCATE COMMUNITY SERVICE OPPORTUNITIES

Some of the youth that your program can reach are those who are sentenced by the juvenile court system to give a certain number of hours of community service. Contact the people in charge to find out what kinds of service you can provide for these youth to fulfill the court's requirement. Then make your church and its ministry available to these youth.

Often these at-risk youth need love, support, and affirmation—qualities your church youth group can provide. When these youth perform community service at your church, you can let them know about the programs you offer.

Go one step further. Arrange to have an adult be with the juveniles during their service time—showing them how to work some of the equipment and to do some of the work. Perhaps a mentoring relationship will begin.

17 VISIT PTA MEETINGS

One great way to let unchurched teens know what's going on inside your church is by letting their parents know. Any place you can meet and get to know parents of youth outside your church is an opportunity for reaching unchurched youth. Get to know the parents at the local PTA, for example. As parents look for ways to keep their teenagers busy and active, they'll remember the programs you've mentioned at those meetings.

18 HOLD A SCAVENGER HUNT

Whether it's a

• video scavenger hunt,

• a Polaroid® scavenger hunt,

• a kidnapping (where youth "kidnap" other youth to go out for ice cream or some other snack),

• a canned food hunt supplying the local food bank,

when the youth go through the neighborhood in groups representing the youth ministry of your church, they will be visible.

A scavenger hunt can be lots of fun, especially if the things being searched for are creative and unique. This is a great way to get other youth in your community to see your youth having fun.

19 HANG UP FLYERS AT HANGOUTS

When you plan a big event (a dance, a fall kick-off, a retreat) make sure that other youth know about it. Take flyers out to the places those youth hang out. Have someone

- hand out flyers at a mall parking lot,
- distribute flyers about a dance to youth coming out of a stadium after a football game,
- give calendars of the summer schedule to the teenagers at the local park.

In public schools in some states, youth are allowed to hand out flyers in their schools. Make sure that you print the telephone number of the church or of a youth leader so that youth and their parents can get more information.

34

20 CREATE T-SHIRTS

When an event is over, you want youth to not only remember what happened but to talk about it with other youth. For an added cost of usually less than ten dollars per person, you can supply t-shirts for your youth. Customize the design. Ask a youth who is creative to design a shirt for the event. Youth can also work in small teams with some supplying ideas and feedback for the one who actually creates the art.

Also consider printing a youth group shirt to be available for anyone. Don't wait for an event!

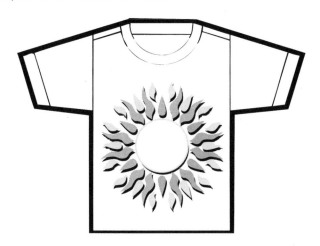

IDEAS THAT ATTRACT NEW YOUTH

Once they're informed about what's happening in your youth ministry program, how should you get unchurched teens to come and keep coming? **Remember:**

> The success of any program relies on the enthusiasm of the active youth and adult leaders.

Since most visitors first come to a youth program as a result of an invitation from another youth, getting your youth involved in the following programs and events will add to their enthusiasm.

1 COMPETE

Have a contest with your youth to see who can bring the most friends. Plan an event that is full of wild and fun activities about which your kids can get excited. As an added incentive, find someone who will shave a beard or cut his or her hair if the number of new people hits a certain amount.

Make sure that you plan good follow-up for this event so that the visitors will be visited and welcomed back by youth.

Ideas That Attract New Youth

2 PLAN MEANINGFUL PROGRAM TOPICS

Lead programs on self-esteem and on topics that help others feel good about themselves. Unchurched kids often need affirmation and acceptance. Make sure that your programs are energetic and creative, using resources that actively involve youth.

3 COFFEE, ANYONE?

Try offering an open coffee house after school. Youth want a safe place to hang out, get homework done, kick back, and have coffee or a soda. You don't always need to have a program and activity planned.

Sometimes the best

ministry is done without

an agenda.

4 RISE AND SHINE

Cook and serve breakfast before school one morning every week, offering to get kids to school on time. It's a great way to start off the day, and it's not difficult to prepare a breakfast each week. End with a short devotion given by a youth, a guest from the congregation, the minister, or you. Offer prayer for any joys and concerns the youth may have.

Make sure that you get the youth to school on time each week. You can find adults to volunteer to drive the youth, giving other adults a way to minister to the students too.

As the breakfasts become more and more regular, the youth of your church will trust that they can invite their unchurched friends.

5 LET'S PARTY!

Plan dances or parties with a theme, inviting the youth of the community. While these don't have to be monthly, a regular schedule does help youth know what to expect and when. Hire a disc jockey, get your youth to decorate, and get the word out through ads, flyers, and word of mouth.

Offer a "Fifth Quarter" event after local football games where youth can come and hang out, eat, dance, and have fun. At each party make sure that you use your creativity to announce what's coming up for the youth.

6 BREAK THE ICE

Begin each event with an ice breaker, enabling youth to feel more comfortable with one another. A newcomer wants to feel welcome right away. Plan a short game that will mix the youth and get people talking with one another. It doesn't have to go with the program (although it helps).

Starting off with an ice breaker or mixer also helps everyone focus on what's happening now rather than on the numerous things that have gone on in the past week.

7 TAKE A ROAD TRIP

Plan some day events that involve traveling in large vehicles. Spending time in a van with other youth helps foster fellowship and allows people to get to know one another better. Get some of your youth to plan these trips so that they take ownership and get excited about the event.

The more excitement—

the more they'll

tell others what's

happening.

8 THE HUNT IS ON

Different types of scavenger hunts are ways to build excitement in your own regular youth and, in turn, build excitement in new youth. Here are some things to remember about scavenger hunts:

• Put an adult with each group.

• Keep group size down so that each group fills up no more than one vehicle.

• Print out clear instructions and give them to each group.

• Give a clear beginning and ending time as well as boundaries.

• Don't repeat a hunt too often.

Use creativity—Polaroid® hunts, video, used clothing, canned food, and people scavenger hunts are all excellent varieties of this activity.

9 ENCOURAGE NEW YOUTH TO PARTICIPATE ON WEEKEND RETREATS

A weekend retreat brings youth to a meaningful relationship with other Christians and with Christ. At a recent conference, one thousand Christian teenagers were asked what single event did the most to bring them to a decision to follow Christ. The number one answer was a retreat.

There are good reasons why a retreat can be so powerful. Even in the Bible you will find accounts of people being fed spiritually when they retreated from the crowds and the regular stresses of the day to reflect on God's calling and direction for their lives.

God takes those opportunities and makes them into huge faith steps.

Encouraging your youth—especially your new, unchurched youth—to go on an upcoming retreat is a great opportunity for growth.

Make sure that you have all the information and registration printed on a flyer that you can hand to the new youth. Then have two youth give him or her a call asking if he or she will go on the retreat. Call the parents too. Answer any questions they may have about the retreat; assure them of their child's safety and possible spiritual growth.

10 MAKE A FOLLOW-UP CALL

Find an active youth who will call the visitor and invite him or her back to the next meeting. A visiting youth is much more likely to return when invited back personally within the first week after the visit. If that call is made by another youth, the visiting youth is even more likely to come back than if an adult calls.

Create a follow-up team that will commit to calling every visitor between 2-5 days after the visit. Ask members of that team to offer the visitor a ride to the next youth meeting.

11 DEVELOP VISION AND SKILLS

Help your active youth become excited and interested in attracting and keeping new youth. The vision statement for your church's youth ministry should contain words about reaching new youth. Help the youth who are leaders in your youth group claim that vision as their own. Lead a planning day to educate active youth on the need for reaching out to unchurched youth. Teach them skills for inviting. Give them opportunity for practicing there, in a safe environment.

Help these youth make a goal to bring in an attainable number of new youth in the next year. Then, at the end of the year, hold a special rally for those who made the commitment and for all the new youth who joined your youth group in that past year.

12 PLAN EVENTS FOR SERVICE

Plan events that reach out to the community, allowing local unchurched youth to volunteer to help and get interested in what's happening. Some suggestions—

- an Advent festival with crafts and art available for children to enjoy

- a haunted house around Halloween and All Saints Day

- a "fun run" for a charity

- Vacation Bible School leaders

- local mission projects

As unchurched youth hear about the event, they may volunteer to help. As they volunteer, they may feel more at ease coming to other youth events.

13 BE WILD AND CRAZY

Do something crazy or unexpected and you will draw kids back from the edge. A friend or group of friends will tell their unchurched buddies a crazy story about all the fun they have at a church youth program and invite them, bringing newcomers in the door again and again.

14 GATHER IN SMALL GROUPS

Plan small group ministry with your churched youth, incorporating an "open chair" in their groups and asking "Whom do you know who needs this small group?" As the members of the small group identify other youth and pray for them, their own sensitivity to others' need for the church will grow. Then inviting them into the group will follow.

Small group ministry can be a highly-effective way to bring others into the church. It begins by plugging youth into an accountability/support group that will focus on taking care of one another.

15 DEVELOP TOOLS OF EVANGELISM

Teach your youth who are leaders how to "evangelize" to other unchurched friends while still accepting them for where they are in their faith—not requiring a change or commitment in order to come to the basic youth group meetings.

16 PLAY MUSIC

Music is a large part of what is important to an adolescent. Have high-energy music playing when things are starting and close with music in a short worship time. Youth may find themselves humming a tune in the middle of the week that reminds them of what went on last Sunday.

17 MAKE IT EASY TO INVITE

Create a safe place and time where your active youth trust what is happening, are informed about what's coming up, and feel comfortable inviting their unchurched friends. This should be a weekly fellowship event with no heavy pressure, no embarrassment, no emotional strings, no expectations of faith or biblical knowledge. This entry-level event will be an easy beginning and a comfortable place for new youth as they determine just what other avenues of ministry they would like to try at your church.

18 BE YOURSELF

Youth can

recognize what's

fake.

19 RESPECT YOUTH

Treat all the youth with respect. Don't talk down to them.
Don't insult them. Don't ever lie. Don't repeat things told to
you in confidence. And don't talk about other youth behind
their backs. The respect you'll receive from showing them
respect will help curb discipline problems too.

20 TAKE ATTENDANCE

You need to know when a youth is no longer attending
regularly. Follow up personally. (You may ask another reliable
youth to do so also.) Let that person know that he or she has
been missed.

Some teenagers are so obvious when they are there that
you'll know right away when they are not there. However,
you may not be as aware of new youth who are missing.

If youth know that it's important to you that they come, even
when they have no particular responsibility that night, they
will give extra effort to get there.

LEAP THE BARRIERS

Tom had just found a place where people didn't try to push him around. He was tired of parents, teachers, neighbors, and even friends telling him what to do. He knew that he was unique; so when he was welcomed into First Church's youth group so quickly, despite his nose ring and bleached hair, he felt relief. Finally he had found a place where he could be himself and find fellowship without the pressure.

But one Sunday morning, when Tom decided to try worship for the first time, a woman from the choir rushed up to him immediately after the service; started shaking her finger at him; and said, "You should be ashamed of yourself coming in here dressed like that and looking like that. You have no respect for God or for this church. Why don't you just keep hanging out with others like you instead of coming in here and disturbing decent church folks?"

Tom did not come to worship again.

It's frustrating to set up a ministry that is working and running smoothly and have it undermined! Something as "small" as a comment like the one in Tom's story or a stereotype or rumor can quickly slam the door in the faces of those to whom you are trying to minister.

Church people can be judgmental; some won't like the unchurched invading their safe place.

How to leap this:

- Help your churched youth be real about who they are. Show them how to share their fears, their weaknesses, their questions, their interests, and so forth. Plan mixers before each event in order to build fellowship and friendship.

- Acknowledge to the governing board of your church that it is risky and difficult to open our doors to outsiders who know nothing of our traditions. Explain, though, that if those traditions are to be handed down, there must be others to hand them to.

- Church leaders might enjoy mentoring new youth in the traditions of the church. The mentor could be a youth or an adult. The mentor should check each week with the newcomer to see if he or she needs a ride to the next youth meeting or worship service. The mentor should also pray for the newcomer daily and encourage him or her to register for the next retreat.

- Talk to the leaders in your congregation about the support you need in order to make these new youth comfortable. Keep the entire church informed about what's happening in youth ministry.

Visiting youth are unsure if they are really welcome into a close fellowship of believers.

How to leap this:

- Show the regular youth how to make newcomers—no matter who they are—feel loved and accepted. Do some role plays to help youth gain empathy and skills for welcoming others.

- Organize a committee of youth who will make a point to call visitors within two to five days to invite them back for the next meeting.

MAKE NEW YOUTH FEEL WELCOME

They've received the information; they're even trying your youth group meetings. Now how can you help those new youth feel welcome? They may have no clue how to handle themselves in a church, so there is already an awkwardness between them and your "regular" youth. Here are things to keep in mind:

1 INTRODUCE NEW YOUTH, BUT . . .

Don't put them on the spot by asking them to introduce themselves nor by asking them to tell the group about their most embarrassing moment. Don't single out the visitors.

2 ALLOW FOR SPONTANEITY

Since unchurched youth have no previous church experience, you may need to move away from what's scheduled now and then. (Of course, in youth ministry this is more the norm than not.)

3 DON'T ASSUME KNOWLEDGE OF THE BIBLE OR CHURCH TRADITION

Newcomers, especially, may not know Peter, the prodigal son, or even Jesus. They may think that Moses was on the ark and that Balaam's Donkey is the name of a new rock band. They also may not understand why we show respect in the sanctuary.

You may feel like you're repeating yourself at times, but take care of these new kids. The seeds have just been planted; their faith is very tender.

4 VISIT NEW YOUTH AFTER THEIR INITIAL VISIT

Take a few youth and visit the visitors to invite them back. Discuss what the various youth find attractive in your church and its youth ministry. These early visits would also provide a great opportunity to find out about the needs of the new youth.

5 DISCOVER THEIR TALENTS AND USE THEM AS SOON AS POSSIBLE

When a youth's talent is recognized and used in the youth program, the young person experiences affirmation and a feeling of belonging.

6 DON'T EMBARRASS NEW YOUTH

Hazing or initiation rites that focus on embarrassment are off limits. Present programs in the youth group about welcoming and accepting people, keeping the topic of acceptance of others in the front of your active youths' minds. Practice important skills through role playing how they should and shouldn't welcome new youth into the group.

7 CLOSE WITH AN OPEN CIRCLE

End each youth meeting with a prayer or benediction in an open circle. Tell the youth that the openness of the circle is a reminder that the group is always open for others to enter.

8 KNOW THEIR NAMES

Learn the new youth's name as soon as possible. Try taking pictures of visitors each week and memorizing their name and face in the week following their initial visit.

Remembering a youth's name the second time he or she comes can have a very high impact.

9 GREET YOUTH AS SOON AS THEY COME IN

It's very awkward to stand in the room—holding up the wall all night—and wonder if anyone even notices you are there.

---

10 PAIR UP NEWCOMERS WITH OTHER YOUTH DURING THE ENTIRE MEETING

Pick out those friendly, outgoing youth who will take a newcomer under wing. Introducing the newcomer to some of the friendlier youth helps him or her feel welcome.

11 WATCH YOUR LANGUAGE

Don't say, "I hope you'll visit us again soon."

Rather, say, "I hope you'll become an active part of this group. You have lots to give."

Helping the new youth feel a part of the group quickly will help him or her forget about being a visitor.

12 TELL THE YOUTH ABOUT THE UPCOMING EVENTS

Announce what is coming up, and tell those newcomers that you want to see them at that event. New youth will feel more welcome if they are invited to the next event by other youth as well.

13 HELP NEWCOMERS KNOW WHAT TO EXPECT

Youth who are new don't want to be caught off guard. Take a few minutes extra to invite and answer questions the new person may have. Offer a word or two of explanation even if there are not questions forthcoming. A schedule will also help relieve that stress of not knowing. Of course, this means that you will have to know what's happening, too.

14 BREAK UP INTO SMALL GROUPS AS OFTEN AS POSSIBLE

Discussion goes much easier for newcomers if they don't have to speak up in front of a large group. They also get to know others more quickly in small groups.

15 MAIL BIRTHDAY CARDS

If you are keeping track of who is visiting, you should also be keeping information like addresses, phone numbers, parent names, and birthdays. It's a great surprise when a youth gets an unexpected birthday card from someone. Make a habit of sending out birthday cards every Monday to those who have birthdays coming up the next week.

Show new youth who Christ is

What makes the church youth group different from any other youth organization? How is what you do in your youth ministry different than what is done in a school key club, a Boy Scout troop, a Junior Civitans meeting, or a group of close friends who get together once a week? Well, there may be a number of differences, but the major difference is that the church youth group is bound together by a mission to bring the gospel of Jesus Christ to youth through the support of the Holy Spirit as it works in the church.

So it is always a goal to bring every youth—unchurched as well as those who have grown up in the church—to a personal relationship with Jesus. Each person is unique, and so his or her relationship is unique. Each person has a different faith process. Some are ready for a deeper faith much sooner than others. This growth is something that involves the Holy Spirit more than it involves you and other youth leaders.

Nevertheless, it is important to help the youth in your group recognize Jesus as he works in and through their lives. This involves helping the youth study and understand God's Word for their lives, pointing them toward service of others, and guiding them in spiritual disciplines where the movement of the Holy Spirit can more easily be recognized.

The following are some ways you can introduce and nurture your youth to a relationship with Jesus Christ:

1 ENCOURAGE YOUTH TO PARTICIPATE ON SPIRITUAL RETREATS

Retreats can bring youth to a meaningful relationship with Christ. (See page 44.)

2 BECOME A CHRONICLER OF THE ACTS OF THE HOLY SPIRIT IN YOUR GROUP

It's not always easy for a person to see how God works in his or her own life. Sometimes people need someone who will make connections between God's work and what is happening in their lives. Perhaps you can be that person—or maybe you know of a church member who has this gift.

Chronicling involves

storytelling (true stories),

some insight, and

permission from the youth

when a story evolves that begs

to be told.

As the youth hear how God is working in their own lives, they too will come to recognize God alive in the world around them.

3 HELP YOUTH DISCOVER THEIR SPIRITUAL GIFTS

The Holy Spirit gives each person gifts that are to be used to glorify God and to promote Christ's church. Helping your youth recognize these gifts will shed new light on how they can make an impact in their church and in their community.

> When they realize the gift, they are more likely to acknowledge the giver—God.

You can find lists of these gifts in Romans 12:6 and in chapters 12 through 14 of First Corinthians.

4 CLOSE OUT EACH TIME WITH WORSHIP

Youth will recognize the importance that you put on worship when they see that it plays a main role in their meeting time—whether that is Sunday school or fellowship time. Getting them involved in the worship leadership will help them take ownership and link their faith with community worship.

5 SURPRISE NEW YOUTH WITH LOVE AND KINDNESS

The word *agape* is a Greek word for *love*—the kind of love that is Christian love. Help your youth understand who God is by helping them experience God's love. Here are some ideas that will knock their socks off:

- The week following the newcomer's arrival, and with his or her parents' permission, throw a Tuesday evening surprise party for the newcomer at his or her house. This involves the parents too, allowing you to work with them and giving them a chance to meet you and the other youth.

- Send the newcomer a balloon bouquet at school.

- Decorate his or her locker.

- Have youth and adults in the church send affirming letters to the home address.

- Have a Sunday school class be in charge of a cookie plate or munchie basket to take by the new youth's house the week after the first visit.

MiNi - WORKSHOP

Use this workshop outline to train the leaders in your church—adults and youth—on the importance, the difficulties, the challenges, and the rewards of opening your church doors to unchurched youth.

The more youth and adults

you have involved—

the more excitement and support toward

bringing in outsiders

to youth ministry—

the more everyone owns the ministry.

	minutes

- WELCOME   5–15
  —Begin with a mixer to help bridge
    some gaps, ending in small groups
    of no more than six.
  —Read page 41 to emphasize the importance
    of mixers.

- BIBLE STUDY/DEVOTION (pages 7–14)   15–20
  — Have small groups read Bible
    references and determine how
    that Scripture relates to opening
    our doors to the unchurched.

- WHO ARE THE UNCHURCHED YOUTH?   10–15
  (pages 15–16)
  — Discuss the status
    questions and where
    youth hang out in your
    community.

	minutes

• WHAT CAN WE DO TO ATTRACT THEM?   10–15
 (pages 32-47)
 —Ask small groups to choose two or three
 of the ideas (or add their own) that they can
 see working for your church. Have each
 group present their thinking to the others.

• HOW DO WE WELCOME THEM?   15–20
 (pages 48-50)
 —Role play the barriers and discuss how
 those barriers can be crossed.
 —Role play some of the ideas that help youth
 feel welcomed (pages 56-61).

• HOW CAN WE SHOW GOD   10–15
 WELCOMING THEM? (pages 62-67)
 —Tell stories of experiences.
 —Discuss how to carry out particular ideas.

• COME UP WITH A PLAN FOR THE NEXT YEAR   10–15

• CLOSING   5–10
 —Use the open circle (page 59).

THE BIG PICTURE

Working with youth is a little like putting together a jigsaw puzzle: It helps to have a picture of what it's supposed to look like! (See page 73.)

In effective youth ministry **vision** is central.

Seven major elements contribute to realizing that vision. The more of them that are developed and in place, the better.

Youth ministry planners in individual churches can develop each of those areas **their own way**, according to their congregation's particular resources, gifts, and priorities and the needs of their youth.

How does this SkillAbility fit in this big picture? Here are just a few of the ways. By using ideas in this book, not only do you open doors and open arms to youth who have not had a relationship to the church and to Christ, you also

- give youth skills for witnessing to their friends and others in the **COMMUNITY;**

- provide **STRUCTURE** that makes it easier for youth to invite and for new youth to feel comfortable and connected;

- create an **ETHOS** of welcoming love that makes a safe place for hungry and hurting, lost and lonely teens to discover God's care for them;

- honor youth with your **PERSPECTIVE** of them as partners and leaders with gifts, which they can share with others.

YOUTH MINISTRY: A COMPREHENSIVE APPROACH

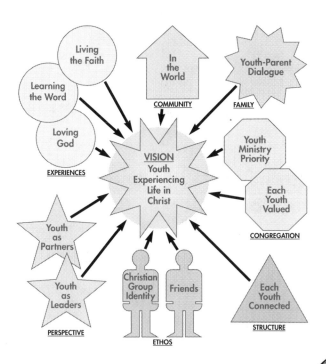

FAMILY

Research is clear that **parent-youth dialogue** about matters of faith is crucial for youth to develop mature faith. Youth themselves express desire to be listened to, to have boundaries, and to have parental involvement in their lives. Parents need skills for relating to their changing teens as well as assurance that their values and voice do matter to their youth. How do we in the church facilitate parent-youth dialogue?

Youth-Parent Dialogue

Communication

Faith Sharing

Arenas

Listened To

Involvement

CONGREGATION

Youth ministry is the ministry of the whole congregation, beginning with making **youth ministry a priority**: prayer for the ministry, people (not just one person), time, effort, training, resources, and funding. The goal for the congregation is **each youth valued**. Interaction with adults, including mentors, positive language about youth, prayer partners for each one, simply being paid attention to—these are active roles for the congregation.

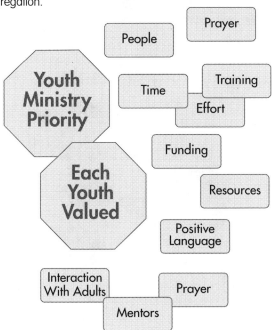

STRUCTURE

Whatever shape the ministry takes, the goal is to have **each youth connected**. Sunday school and youth group are only a beginning. What are the needs of the youth? What groups (even of only 2 or 3 youth) and what times would help connect young people to the faith community? How easy is it for new youth to enter? How well do we stay in touch with the changing needs of our youth? Do we have structures in place that facilitate communication? outreach? "How" can vary; it's the "why" that's crucial.

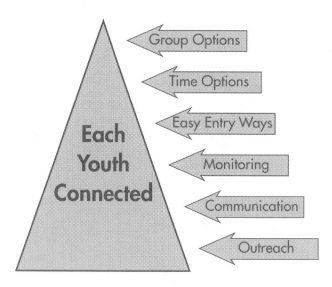

ETHOS

We are relational beings; we all need **friends**. The support, caring, and accountability friends provide help youth experience the love of God. As those friendships are nurtured within **Christian group identity**, young people claim for themselves a personal identity of being Christian. What language, rituals, traditions, and bonding experiences mark each grouping within the youth ministry as distinctively Christian?

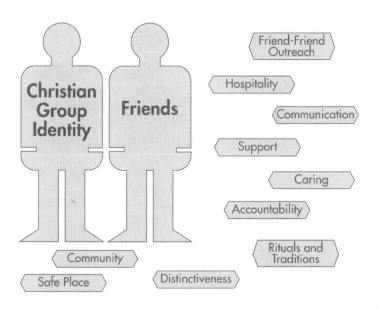

PERSPECTIVE

Youth are keenly aware of being seen as problems, being treated as objects to be fixed, or as recipients too inexperienced to have anything to offer. What would happen if we operated from the perspective of seeing **youth as leaders, youth as partners**? We would listen to them more, be intentional about identifying their gifts, take seriously their input, encourage their decision making, and train them for leadership roles.

Youth
as
Partners

Serving Others

Serving With Adults

Opportunities

Trained

Gifts Identified

Youth
as
Leaders

Decision-Making Roles

Encouraged

Input

Open Doors, Open Arms

EXPERIENCES

Worship, devotions, prayer, and participation in the community of faith build for youth the experience of **loving God**. Study and reflection upon the Bible and the faith are crucial for **learning the Word**. Being among people who are Christian role models and grappling with difficult moral, ethical, justice, and stewardship issues help young people with **living the faith**. Curriculum resources specifically provide material to facilitate these three kinds of experiences.

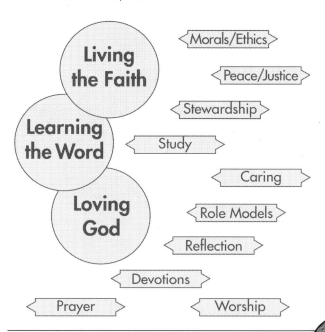

COMMUNITY

As Christians, youth are challenged to be **in the world** as servants, as witnesses, as leaven—making a difference with their lives, giving others a glimpse of the Kingdom. What opportunities, what training, what support do we give youth to equip them for ministry beyond the walls of the church building?

In
the
World

Serving

Witnessing

Leaven/Salt/Light